love
like
arson

poems by
jessica katoff

LOVE LIKE ARSON
BY JESSICA KATOFF

ISBN-10: 099031801X
ISBN-13: 978-0-9903180-1-9
First Print Edition, 2014

10 9 8 7 6 5 4 3 2 1

CONNECT WITH JESSICA

jessicakatoff.com
jessicakatoff@gmail.com
facebook.com/jessicakatoff
twitter.com/jessicakatoff
goodreads.com/jessicakatoff
instagram.com/jessicakatoff

To purchase signed copies and exclusive typewritten, handbound versions of this book, selected typewritten poems, and other exclusives from Jessica Katoff, please visit:

ETSY.COM/SHOP/JESSICAKATOFF

DEDICATION

P, if these words ever find you, I hope you know this is a book I never wanted to write. I just didn't know how else to release this pain, other than to bleed all over these pages. I miss you and I'm sorry.

TABLE OF CONTENTS

PART I: KINDLING

PART II: FLAMES

PART III: ASHES

part i:
kindling

001

She was the kind of girl
who never needed love,
but that didn't mean
she wouldn't long for it.

I will admit,
you terrified me,
because I had never
known another person,
besides myself,
who believed
in such honesty,
and I spent so long
lying to myself
about your very existence.

003

You were so far
out of my reach,
but my heart ran all of those
merciless miles,
straight into your arms,
and never looked back.

004

You kissed me,
and, my heart,
so long dead
in my chest,
cracked open,
and love bloomed
all around us,
birthed from the
pieces we broke free.

Falling for you was effortless,
an action as natural as gravity.
When each new day would breach the blinds,
and shine its newborn rays into my eyes,
I would see you in the glow,
the brightest star I ever found.
How could the planet of my heart
have escaped your pull, when the mere
presence of you pinned me to the ground?

006

I am never lost,
nor ever found,
for all roads lead to you.

007

The moonlight laid
across your skin,
its silvery hands
spreading wide
across your hips
and gliding slowly
down your throat,
and though I tried to
trace the pathways
it lit for me,
my hands could never touch
as much as that
celestial body could,
and I knew I would
never have enough.

008

There was no greater feeling
than the softness of our silence
and all the ways it surrounded us
and felt like home.

I don't know when or why
you built your walls so high,
but once I found the places
the light could get in
and saw what was enclosed,
I unearthed a man so great,
I was nearly certain
you only walled yourself off
to save the world from
the terrible beauty you could expose.

010

When I told you there was
a darkness within me,
you told me you'd be
the light,
and of what a beautiful
sunrise we would make.

011

I have never been an optimist,
but there was something about you
that made me see years into the future,
and that world, a world with you, was a world
in which I could have lived in bliss.

012

The second our mouths met,
the taste of yours so new,
I swallowed down every notion
about not falling for you.

013

You were the tune
and I, the words,
and together we composed
the sweetest song ever heard.

014

You had a way about you
that made me believe in magic;
I fell for your sleight of hand
and got lost in every illusion.

015

"This has the
potential to hurt,"
you said.
"All the best things do,"
I replied.
But I was never afraid,
because I knew you
would be worth
any amount of pain.

016

If the law of
perpetual motion
is impossible,
explain love.

017

I don't know who
won or lost;
all I know is I
stopped keeping score,
when you caught my lips and
I slid home beneath your skin.

018

You knew how I felt about fate
and the false gods of fake people,
but you crashed into my life,
as Lucifer fell from Heaven,
and the Devil of you
will forever be the closest
I will come to belief.

019

I didn't need saving,
just someone
I wouldn't need to
save myself from.

020

I was always the kind of
person to build homes
on unsteady ground.
So, it's no surprise that
I laid foundation
on your shaking chest
and made my bed
in your trembling hands.

What a
sweet suffering
I bear,
to be the one
who loves you.

part ii: flames

001

Yours is a love like arson;
your only desire
is to burn me down.
And I am your willing pyre,
begging you to light me up.

002

I would take every brutal
ounce of blame,
if it meant you would
look at me the same
way you did,
before you knew
just how many pieces
my past had shattered me into.

003

Tell me now;
let us waste no more time.
Did you ever love me?
Were you ever mine?

004

The universe gave me you,
when I stopped expecting
good things.
But the world is cruel,
and just as easily as it gives,
it takes.
And it does not apologize
for the wreckage it makes.

005

I told myself I wouldn't dwell,
but when I breathe in,
you are what fills my lungs,
and no amount of screaming
will exorcise you from my chest.

006

I found galaxies
in your eyes
and now I can't see
even a single star.

007

The only lie I ever told
was in reply to
the only truth you ever spoke.
"I can't do this anymore," you said.
"I believe you," I replied.

008

You are a man who wants to
leave his mark on the world,
and I will forever be scarred
by what that turned you into.

009

I didn't need
"I love you."
I needed
"It's okay.
I'm here.
I won't leave you."

010

It is devastating to know
I am so easy to let go.

011

There are millions of words
about broken hearts,
including my own,
but none of them matter,
because none of them change
the fact that you've gone.

012

Tell me how to stop
loving you;
teach me
your effortless ways.

013

I don't know how to
walk these streets
with the ghost of you
trailing behind me.

014

This weary body has felt
pain worse than this,
but not of this kind,
one not of blood, bone, or vein,
but an agony of the heart and mind.

015

The worst thing about
heartbreak is that it's
a self-inflicted wound.
After all, wasn't it I
who fell in love with you?

016

You may be gone,
but you left a stain
on everything you
ever touched,
and I can't rid
my skin of your ghost.

017

I have cried
a tear for each hour
I knew you,
and I have
lifetimes more
willing to spill,
if only you would
give me the time.

018

Maybe I should
thank you.
After all, I felt nothing
for so long,
and this pain is
making up for lost time.

019

You can keep your promises;
I don't want them anyway.

020

If there are no words
left to say,
explain why my body language
knows only one phrase;
"I love you."

021

I don't wish you pain
but knowing you hurt
might make my wounds
seem worth having.

022

Falling for you was
more like drowning;
the farther I sank,
the more it hurt,
until the pressure
crushed me completely.

023

What a sinister thing
the mind can be;
it knows this bed is empty,
yet it let you fill my dreams.

024

Is there any combination of
letters or words or phrases
that will grant me enough
forgiveness to hear your mouth
spill anything other than
another goodbye?

025

Questions unanswered
and words unspoken
are the weapons of loss
that left me broken.

026

Nothing goes better with
black coffee than sorrow,
and since you left,
I've spent each morning
drinking cup after
bitter cup.

027

You taught me how to
see the world in color,
but everything is a blur
beyond these
Technicolor tears.

028

When it comes to love,
we all bleed the same way.
And I hope that you're bleeding, too.
I hope this meant something to you.

029

All of our phases were
captured in three-word
phrases:
I like you.
I want you.
I need you.
I love you.
Don't leave me.

030

What else am I to do
with all these memories of you?

031

In the end,
there was no
fixing the things
we destroyed,
and that is why
this is the end,
and not just
another chapter
in the long
and sordid story
of us.

part iii:
ashes

001

I know we both
deserve better,
but I want you
just the same.

002

What hurts the most
is knowing
a man of such strength
was too weak to love
a woman of such weakness,
who loved too strongly.

003

You use phrases like
for now and *one day*
and I hope you know the weight
of the words that you say.

004

My mind keeps
flickering between,
"He was everything
I ever wanted," and
"If that was true,
wouldn't he have
wanted me, too?"

005

I wish I had
written about you
before this
bitterness
took hold.

006

I want for nothing,
but I hope for far too much
to be considered
a truly selfless lover.

007

I would rather
be alone,
than beg for
the attention
of a man
who leaves me
lonely.

008

How does hope
still flow in these veins,
when you've drained me
of everything else?

009

Maybe it's less about
your broken heart,
and more about the fact
that you were willing to let
someone close enough to
touch your heart
at all.

010

I should have been
less focused on losing you
and more focused on giving
you reasons to stay.

011

There is no illness
quite like loneliness
and no cure
quite like love.

012

I wonder how many
hours will pass before
I stop thinking of you.
I wonder how many
hours are left
in my life.
I wonder which
number is greater.

013

There is no difference between
the woman I was before
and the woman I am now,
unless you look closely enough
to see the tiny cracks in my heart
that spell out your name.

014

All the love in the world
doesn't seem to matter,
if it isn't the kind you want,
from the person you need.

015

There is an endless longing
you've awakened within me
and I don't know how to be
a girl who doesn't
get what she wants.

016

I was too much
and not enough,
for a man
who was everything
and nothing at all.

017

"Give it time"
they say,
but no one tells you
how to get through the days,
without thinking of what
you're waiting to escape.

018

If you ever
remember to miss me,
know that I will
remember to forget.

019

I hope that someday soon,
I'll be able to think of you,
without my chest seizing up
at the briefest reminder
of what could have been.

020

Why is it so easy
to put other people
back together,
when they're broken,
but nearly impossible
to even find
our own pieces,
when we fall apart?

021

I must remember
the good with the bad.
After all, there is a reason
this pain feels so vast,
and that reason is made up
of all the ways I loved you
and everything you were
in the past.

It's so foolish to hope for
something so hopeless.
but isn't that what hope is for –
fools like me, who still think
the world can change,
that people can?
Or is it hopeful
to be so foolish?
Either way, I am a fool,
who hopes for love,
even when all hope of
love is gone.

023

If good things come to those who wait,
I will become a monument to time,
because you are the best thing
I had the pleasure of calling mine.

024

There's no shame in a broken heart;
there's only a tender kind of bravery.
You stared down the unknown and
walked forth with your head held high.
You went to war and
came back changed.
Maybe not for the better,
maybe not this time,
but you're stronger now.
And you're still here,
willing and hopeful and ready
to try again.
And there's no shame
in surviving that.
No, there's no dishonor in
openhearted perseverance.

025

Despite everything,
I would wreck my heart
a million times more,
if we could use
the pieces to build
what we should have
had before.

ABOUT THE AUTHOR

JESSICA KATOFF is a boring CEO by day and a women's fiction novelist and contemporary poet by night. When she isn't pretending to be a professional or staring hopelessly at the blinking cursor on her laptop screen, Jessica loves to marvel at the beauty of live music, traverse the globe, not wear pants, bake tasty things, binge watch television shows, drink whiskey and cheap wine, and sleep—not all at once. Jessica hates ignorance, people who talk during movies or with their mouth full, lima beans, and the word "ooze." A southern Florida native and current resident, she plans on relocating to Georgia with her two very fluffy pooches as soon as possible, and is currently accepting applications for a devastatingly perfect husband in the greater Atlanta area.

Want to know more?
Visit **jessicakatoff.com** or connect with Jessica at:

Facebook | **facebook.com/jessicakatoff**
Twitter | **twitter.com/jessicakatoff**
Goodreads | **goodreads.com/jessicakatoff**
Instagram | **instagram.com/jessicakatoff**

She also accepts love letters at **jessicakatoff@gmail.com**

Made in the USA
San Bernardino, CA
11 February 2016